Feeling Angry

by Helen Frost

Consulting Editor: Gail Saunders-Smith, Ph.D.

Consultant: Erik Willcutt, Ph.D.
Child Clinical Psychologist
Instructor, University of Denver

Pebble Books

an imprint of Capstone Press
Mankato, Minnesota

Pebble Books are published by Capstone Press
151 Good Counsel Drive, P.O. Box 669, Mankato, Minnesota 56002
http://www.capstone-press.com

1 2 3 4 5 6 06 05 04 03 02 01

Library of Congress Cataloging-in-Publication Data
Frost, Helen, 1949–
      Feeling angry/by Helen Frost.
      p. cm.—(Emotions)
      Includes bibliographical references and index.
      Summary: Simple text and photographs describe and illustrate anger and ways
to alleviate it.
      ISBN 0-7368-0668-7
      1. Anger in children—Juvenile literature. [1. Anger.] I. Title. II. Emotions
(Mankato, Minn.)
BF723.A4F76   2001
152.4'7—dc21   00-025021

Note to Parents and Teachers

The Emotions series supports national health education standards related to interpersonal communication and expression of feelings. This book describes and illustrates the feeling of anger. The photographs support emergent readers in understanding the text. The repetition of words and phrases helps emergent readers learn new words. This book also introduces emergent readers to subject-specific vocabulary words, which are defined in the Words to Know section. Emergent readers may need assistance to read some words and to use the Table of Contents, Words to Know, Read More, Internet Sites, and Index/Word List sections of the book.

Table of Contents

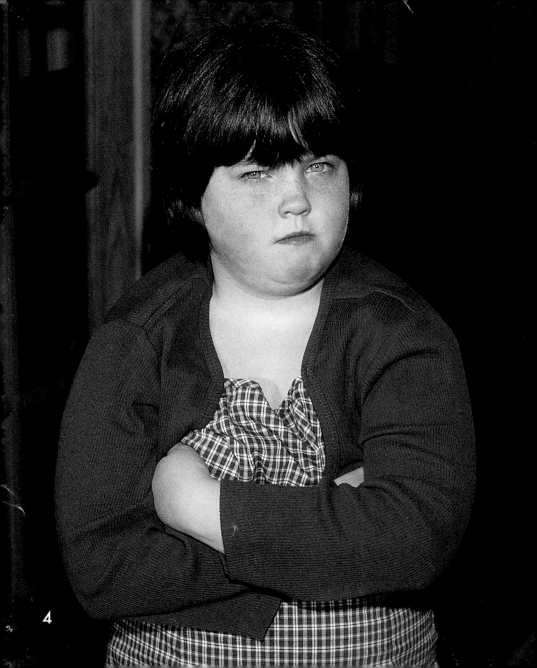

4

You feel mad
when you are angry.

6

Everyone feels

angry sometimes.

You might feel angry
when someone is mean.

You might feel angry
when something is not fair.

You might feel like yelling
when you are angry.

14

You might feel like hitting
when you are angry.

You can learn
to control your anger.

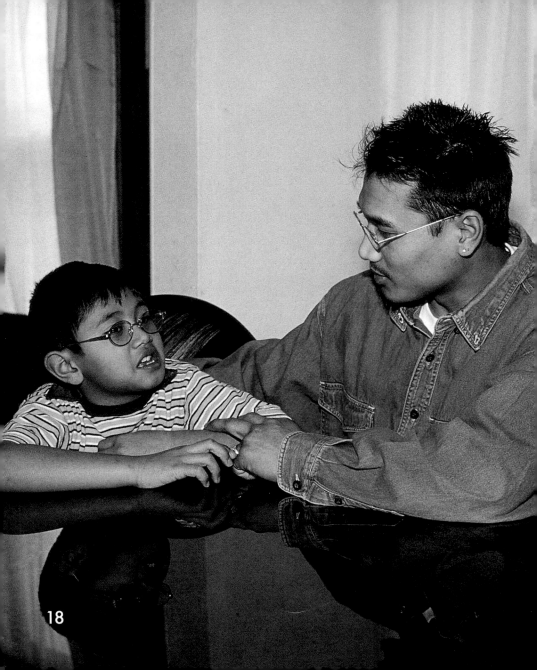

You can talk about
what makes you angry.

You can try to change
what makes you angry.

control—to hold back; people can express anger in ways that do not hurt others.

fair—reasonable and just; people can work to make situations fair.

yell—to shout, cry out, or scream loudly; yelling does not help anger to go away.

Read More

Althea. *Feeling Angry.* Exploring Emotions. Milwaukee: Gareth Stevens Publishing, 1998.

Doudna, Kelly. *I Feel Angry.* How Do You Feel? Minneapolis: Abdo & Daughters, 1999.

Johnson, Julie. *Being Angry.* How Do I Feel About. Brookfield, Conn.: Copper Beech Books, 1999.

Johnston, Marianne. *Dealing with Anger.* The Conflict Resolution Library. New York: PowerKids Press, 1996.

Internet Sites

Dealing With Anger: How to Keep Your Cool
http://www.kidshealth.org/kic/feeling/anger.html

Helping Young Children Cope with Anger
http://www.nncc.org/Guidance/dc31_cope.anger.html

Mister Rogers' Neighborhood: How Do You Feel?
http://www.pbs.org/rogers/make_believe/feel.htm

Rules for Getting Your Mads Out
http://members.aol.com/angriesout/kids.htm

Index/Word List

anger, 17
change, 21
control, 17
everyone, 7
fair, 11
feel, 5, 7, 9, 11,
  13, 15
hitting, 15

learn, 17
mad, 5
mean, 9
someone, 9
something, 11
sometimes, 7
talk, 19
yelling, 13

Word Count: 70
Early-Intervention Level: 6

Editorial Credits
Mari C. Schuh, editor; Kia Bielke, designer; Katy Kudela, photo researcher

Photo Credits
David F. Clobes, 6, 18
Jack Glisson, 1
K. D. Dittlinger, 10
Kim Stanton, 8, 12, 14, 16
Matt Swinden, 20
Unicorn Stock Photos/B. W. Hoffmann, cover
Visuals Unlimited/Eric Anderson, 4

The author thanks the children's section staff at the Allen County Public Library in Fort Wayne, Indiana, for research assistance.